D0531987

Public Library
tt, Arizona

WITHDRAWN

# ROBOTS AMONG US

## THE CHALLENGES
## AND PROMISES OF ROBOTICS

CHRISTOPHER W. BAKER

NEW CENTURY TECHNOLOGY

THE MILLBROOK PRESS
BROOKFIELD, CONNECTICUT

Cover photograph courtesy of Honda Motor Corp., Ltd.
Photographs courtesy of: Tiger Electronics: pp. 3, 46; NASA Ames Research Center: pp. 4, 20; NASA/JPL/Caltech: pp. 6, 7, 8, 19 (right), 22, 23, 42; Triumf, Inc.: p. 9; Robotics Institute/Carnegie Mellon University: pp. 10, 11 (left), 24, 35; Probotics: p. 11 (right); MIT Leg Laboratory/Gil Pratt: pp. 12, 45; Shell Oil and Textron: p. 13; Space Systems Lab/University of Maryland: pp. 14, 30; MIT Artificial Intelligence Lab/Rodney Brooks: pp. 19 (left), 29, 37; iRobot Corporation: p. 21; © V.A. Medical Center/Phototake: p. 26; Robotic Embedded Systems Laboratory/University of Southern California: p. 27; Oak Ridge National Laboratory: p. 33; Duke University: p. 34; Northeastern University Marine Science Center: p. 36; Sandia National Laboratories: pp. 38, 43; Lawrence Livermore National Laboratory: p. 39; © Lipson & Pollack, 2000: p. 40.


Published by The Millbrook Press, Inc.
2 Old New Milford Road
Brookfield, Connecticut 06804
www.millbrookpress.com


Library of Congress Cataloging-in-Publication Data
Baker, Christopher W.
Robots among us : the challenges and promises of robotics / Christopher W. Baker.
p. cm. — (New century technology)
Includes index.
Summary: Describes the development of various types of robots, the challenges inherent in making them more and more complex, and uses of robots now and in the future.
ISBN 0-7613-1969-7 (lib. bdg.)
1. Robots—Juvenile literature. [1. Robots. 2. Automata.] I. Title. II. Series.
TJ211.2 .B35 2002    629.8'92—dc21    2001026702

Copyright © 2002 by Christopher W. Baker
All rights reserved
Printed in Hong Kong
5 4 3 2 1

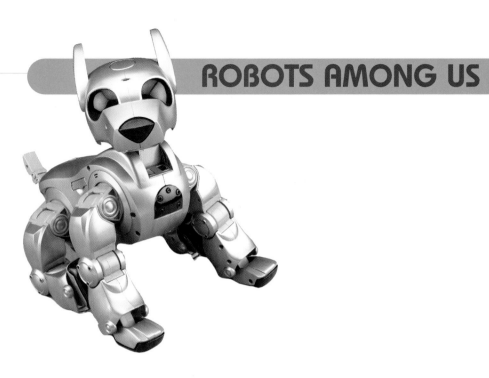

Note the quarter lying next to NASA's latest Nanorover. This miniaturized light-weight rover is a potential candidate for future planetary exploration.

# WHY ROBOTS?

Take a moment to think about what you like doing each day. It may be playing sports, seeing friends at school, exploring nature, learning new things, or playing music in a band. Whatever it is, most of us do some things every day that we would like to spend more time doing.

Now think of the harder parts of every day. How about lugging your overweight backpack, stuffed with school books, from class to class? Or doing chores at home? You may be expected to help clean the house, mow the lawn, or empty the trash. Doesn't it seem that these tasks always pop up just when you're ready to do something you like?

What if you never had to do these things again? Think about what it would be like if you had your own special assistant, someone who would never tire of doing whatever you asked, whenever you asked it. With a robot, in other words, life could be a lot more fun!

Old munitions may be explosive and must be disassembled. To protect people and to speed the process, scientists at Sandia Laboratories in New Mexico designed this robot to handle several rounds at a time.

# ROBOTIC PROMISES

It is natural to want to be freed from the drudgeries of daily life. Yet the promise of robots is actually much larger than just helping us with our chores.

Robots can do many things humans can't do or can't do well. They can, for example, plug chips into circuit boards, weld car bodies on an assembly line, or paint stealth fighter planes more precisely and at speeds far higher than any human can achieve. What's more, they can repeat the same sets of movements over and over again without any worries of injury. If a robot's wrist joint starts to wear out, for example, a technician can simply replace it. An injured human wrist, on the other hand, might require delicate surgery and a long, painful recovery.

Robots also never get bored. Just imagine crawling across the huge metal skin of a 747 jumbo jet looking for tiny cracks in the aluminum. If not detected and repaired, these cracks could lead to major tears during flight and maybe even a crash. Staying alert and fresh for such a large and tedious task is extremely difficult for any human. A robot, however, can methodically inspect every inch of an aircraft's surface with unfailing dedication, making flight safer for everyone.

Robots are never bored. Here we see a robot designed to inspect the aluminum skin of a commercial jet. It is being tested on a loop of metal.

Left: On their own private replica of Mars, scientists from the Jet Propulsion Lab (JPL) test their latest planetary rover. The mast holding its stereo cameras is fully extended to give the rover a better view of its surroundings.

Below: The rover's sample-collecting arm takes a soil sample.

8

In addition, robots can go places we can't go and do things that are too dangerous for humans. Telerobotic robots (which are directly operated by humans using controls located elsewhere) have dived to the bottom of the ocean and discovered the wreck of the *Titanic*. They have traveled to Mars and explored the surface of our neighboring planet. They have dropped into volcanoes to collect samples of deadly gases. They have also been used by police departments to defuse bombs and by environmental cleanup crews to handle toxic spills and radiation leaks.

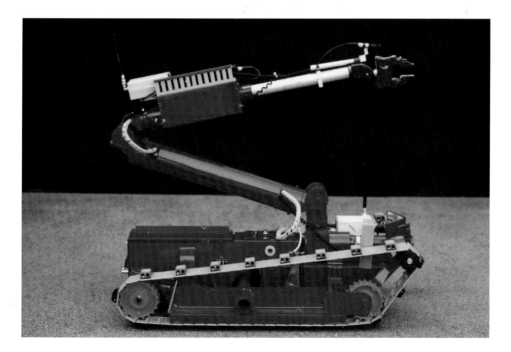

TRIUMF's RoV robot, designed by Hovey, began its life as a bomb-disposal system. It is narrow enough to fit down aircraft aisles and can reach into the upper bins. It has since been adapted to handle radioactive substances in areas that are dangerous for humans to enter.

## Into the Inferno

A robot named Dante II has been to hell and back. Dante II is an eight-legged robot, built by Carnegie Mellon University, that in 1994 descended to collect gas samples inside the active volcanic cone of Mount Spurr in Alaska's Aleutian Mountain Range. Collecting such samples is extremely dangerous, as evidenced by the 1993 deaths of eight vulcanologists in two separate incidents.

Dante II rappelled down the sheer cliff sides of the fumarole (volcanic gas vent) and landed on the floor of the crater, where it gathered and analyzed high-temperature gases. Though it eventually slipped and fell on its side, Dante proved that robots could do useful science in harsh environments without endangering human lives.

Dante II marches bravely over the edge of the crater and into the depths of the Mount Spurr volcano.

Robots are also starting to enter our homes. There are now basic robots that can fetch your soda, vacuum your floors, or keep watch over your property when you are away, as well as robots to entertain us in the form of mechanized dogs, cats, and sophisticated baby doll toys.

In short, robots are affecting our lives in countless ways. Their ultimate promise is their incredible power to extend our abilities as human beings and free us from many difficult and dangerous tasks.

## LOOK SHARP

What do you think a robot should look like? Close your eyes for a moment and try to create a picture of one in your head. Chances are, the image in your mind looks somewhat like a human. This is not surprising, given the many humanoid robots we've seen in films and on television, and read about in books.

"Mechanical humans" have appeared in film and fiction since the 1890s, but they were actually not called robots until a Czech writer, Karel Čapek (pronounced "chop eck"), wrote a popular play in 1921 entitled *R. U. R.*, which stands for "Rossum's Universal Robots." The word "robot" comes from a Czech word, *robota*, which means "forced labor."

**Put on a happy face! Flo has appeared on the *Today* show and is an early design in CMU's Nursebot project. The project's goal is to create personal service robots for the elderly and chronically ill.**

**A new addition to the family? Probotics Inc. has created CYE to help with the household chores. It can fetch and carry things like drinks and newspapers, as well as vacuum and patrol any floor of the house.**

11

In the heart of the MIT Leg Laboratory, a new robot takes shape. Researchers there are building a humanoid, two-legged robot called M2. It is designed to walk fast and be extremely reliable. In the background, hanging from the ceiling, you can see an earlier robot known as Spring Flamingo.

Your human-like picture is also not surprising because you naturally understand that robots, in order to be effective at many of the tasks we would like them to perform, must be capable of functioning in a world that was built by humans for humans. To do so, they must see as we see, or, even better, hear and understand what we say. They must be able to do work with their arms, hands, or other appendages, know where they are, and get where they want to go—up stairs, around obstacles, and across many different kinds of surfaces.

Unfortunately, all of these very human functions that we take for granted are actually highly complex and difficult for robot builders to duplicate in a robot. That is why robots today don't look human at all. Instead, they are designed specifically to fit the tasks for which they are needed.

Some robots are just arms on a stationary stand, perfect for picking parts from a bin and placing them on an assembly line. Others look like mobile platforms with sets of wheels or legs, suited to exploring other planets. And still others look like fish, minisubmarines, or even engine pistons, and are suited to their specific

Shell Oil and Textron collaborated to produce the first fully automated gas pump. The robot opens your tank, fills it up, and away you go without lifting a finger.

duties. Adding anything extra, like legs or wheels on a robot arm, only makes the system more complex, costly, and difficult to manage.

This does not mean that robots will never look and act like us. In fact, considerable research is being done with this idea in mind. It just means there are still a large number of very complex problems that must first be overcome.

## Tying Your Shoes

Let's do a brief experiment to illustrate some of the difficulties faced by roboticists (people who create robots) trying to build robots that can do even seemingly simple tasks. You will need an assistant, so grab a friend or a family member. First, untie one of your shoes but don't take it off. Next, find two pairs of pliers and hold one in each hand. Then, put on a blindfold.

Your job is to be a robot and follow the commands of your assistant to tie your shoe using the pliers. Your assistant can't just tell you to grab a shoelace in each pair of pliers. Where are the laces? How can you find them? The assistant must give you precise directions. "Lower your right hand until the pliers touch the floor. Slide the pliers to the left until you feel a lace. Clamp the pliers on the lace." And much, much more.

Let's say you are finally able to grab the laces. Now the fun really begins as you try to tie a knot. Laces get dropped. Pliers bang into each other. Chaos rules. See how far you can get, but don't be surprised if you can't finish the job at all. Can you begin to see why task-specific robot designs might be necessary? Even seemingly simple tasks can become very difficult from the robot's point of view.

The Supplemental Camera and Maneuvering Platform (SCAMP) is a free-flying robotic camera built to give astronauts and ground control crews better views of what is happening at space station worksites and during EVA excursions. Here we see it being tested in the Space Systems Laboratory's neutral buoyancy tank.

## ACT NATURALLY

How do you think a robot should act? Right away you might say, "Like a human," which is not a bad place to start. But what do we mean by "like a human"? Let's think about ourselves for a moment and see if we can capture some basic behavioral process that guides what we do. If we can discover this, then perhaps we can use it as the basis for robot behavior.

The truth is, very few of us ever stop to examine how we do the things we do every day, from getting dressed to walking, drinking, eating, and more. So let's take a closer look.

Sit at a table with a glass of your favorite juice in front of you, your hands at your sides, and your eyes and head turned away from the glass. Now begin the process of taking a drink. What do you do?

First, you have to locate the glass, so you move your head and eyes until you see the glass before you. As you sweep your eyes across the table, your brain is testing the information your eyes are sending to it, trying to recognize a glass. Finally, you see the glass, and you stop searching. Now you need to decide how to get the glass from the table to your mouth.

Your brain quickly works out a plan, deciding whether to use two hands or one, how to reach out your hand and grab the glass, and then how to raise it to your lips.

15

## The Big Picture

*The sense-think-act cycle is the basic process most robot builders use to control the behavior of their robots. Three essential hardware components make the cycle happen: sensors, a computer processor, and actuators.*

*The sensors, such as cameras, microphones, or touch devices, act like eyes, ears, or skin, taking in information from the surrounding world and sending it to the computer. The computer, like a brain, processes this information, makes plans and decisions, and sends signals to the actuators. The actuators operate like muscles to move the various parts of the robot as directed by the computer.*

*This process repeats at high speed over and over again all the time the robot is switched on, allowing the robot to constantly monitor its world and take action if it is necessary.*

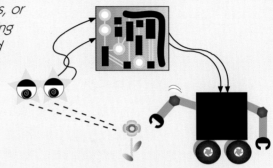

**In a continuously repeating process, sensors send data to a computer, which processes it and makes a decision, sending commands to the actuators, which move the robot.**

Then you spring into action. Your arm lifts up from your side and slides your hand to the glass. You feel the contact with your fingers, close your fingers around the smooth surface, flex the muscles of your arm, and soon you are drinking the sweet, refreshing liquid. This all happens so quickly and so naturally that you normally don't notice it at all.

But if we look closely at what just happened, we can see three distinct steps. First, you sensed your environment (looked for the glass), then you thought about what to do (made a plan to lift the glass to your lips), and finally, you took action (lifted the glass and drank). A somewhat simplified description of the basic cycle of your behavior, then, is sense-think-act. It is this same processing cycle that robot builders use to guide their robots' actions in the world, using it over and over again, just as we do throughout our day.

## BEING SENSITIVE

The first step in the robot's sense-think-act cycle involves taking in information from the surrounding world. Humans do this through their various senses. Take a moment to sense the world around you. Your eyes deliver colors, shapes, and motion. Your ears detect noises both near and far. Your skin feels the clothing lying next to it. Along with smell and taste, these sensations form the rich, full texture of your reality.

Of all these inputs, our primary sense for perceiving the world, in most cases, is sight. It allows us to recognize things at a distance, identify objects, perceive and predict movements, and navigate through our surroundings. Since robots must operate largely within a human-made world, it seems natural that robots should see like we do.

17

As you can see from this diagram, human eyes can perceive only the minutest portion of the electromagnetic spectrum. With the right sensors, robots can "see" much more than we can.

| Gamma-ray | X-ray | Visible | Infrared | Radio |

## Beyond Visible Light

*Visible light is only a very small portion of what is called the electromagnetic spectrum. We humans are limited in what we can sense of this spectrum because of the structure of our eyes. Robots, being machines, are limited only by what we choose to build into them; they could just as easily have "eyes" that can sense infrared, radar, or even X-ray radiations to help them "see" their world. They could even combine sensor systems across the spectrum to get a range of "visible" information not available to our human eyes.*

At first you might think teaching a machine to see would be an easy task: Just mount a camera or two on your robot, feed the images to its processors, and you're done. It sounds simple, but it is actually an extremely difficult process requiring intensive computer calculation.

Machine vision, particularly in robots that must navigate through our human world, often starts with images from two cameras. Can

you guess why? Consider your own visual system. It comes with two eyes for a very good reason. With two eyes, your brain receives two slightly different images of the objects you are looking at. These images are melded together by your brain to give you a feeling of depth, or three-dimensional (3-D) vision.

Robot eyes can work in color, too. Here we see the results of a robot searching for unexploded munitions. It has detected the edges of the shell and can now go to the next stage to decide if it has found what it was looking for.

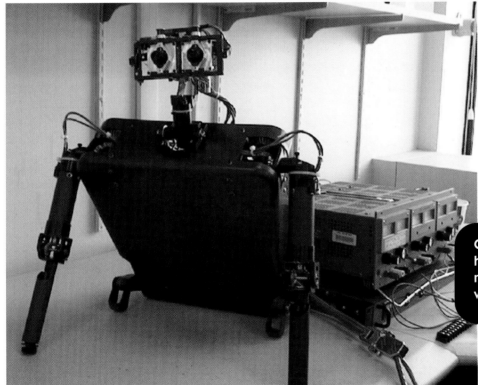

Coco is one of the newest members of the humanoid robotics group at MIT. He is fully mobile and free to explore his environment without the help of a human operator.

19

## Two Eyes, One Image

*Hold a pencil up in front of your face, about an arm's length away. Close your right eye and open your left eye. Then open your right eye and close the left. Do you have the strange feeling that the pencil is moving back and forth before you? What you are seeing is the separate image captured by each eye. Notice that you can see a little more of the right side of the pencil with your right eye, and a little more of the left side of the pencil with your left eye.*

*Notice also that when you use only one eye, the world looks a bit flat. It is harder to judge how far away things are. Now open both eyes. Do you see how the world seems rounder and therefore easier to understand? Your brain has assembled your 3-D visual world from the separate flat images delivered by each eye. This phenomenon is called stereopsis.*

Similarly, computer programs have been developed that can combine paired images from two cameras in order to provide this sort of depth information to a robot. This allows the robot to better understand distance and object location in its world. Yet what good is this depth information if your robot doesn't understand what it is looking at? Somehow, it must also find recognizable shapes in the images given to it by the cameras.

To a robot, a picture is just a collection of tiny rectangular segments called pixels. In any digital image, a pixel is the tiniest unit of visual information. High-resolution images can have many millions of pixels, while low-resolution pictures may have only a few hundred thousand.

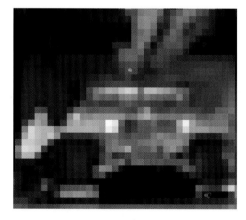

**Notice how when the pixels get really large, it becomes harder to tell what the picture is about? This is one of the reasons that machine vision is so difficult.**

It is important to understand that, in either case, a robot does not have an overview, like we do, of what is in the picture. It has to start at the pixel level and build up a sense of what the image contains. Imagine cutting a photograph into tiny squares and then trying to reconstruct the image in your mind by looking at the squares one at a time. You can begin to realize the difficulties a robot has in understanding what it is seeing.

### *Is One Eye Better Than Two?*

*Although we have been focusing on two-eyed robots up to this point, robots with only one camera are not necessarily less useful. There are actually many situations where a single camera is just as good as two or more. The field of biometrics is a good example.*

*Biometrics literally means "biological measurement" and refers to the precise measurement of various parts of our bodies in order to tell one person from another. For example, no two people's fingerprints are exactly alike, nor the irises in their eyes, nor the structure of their faces (even of identical twins).*

*A single-camera security robot could check the faces of all people entering a building to make sure they are allowed to enter. It would first locate the person's face in the picture, then create a detailed analysis of the face's shape, and then compare it to the face-shape models in its memory. If the shapes match, then the person can enter.*

*In the future, biometric locks on our homes, computers, cars, and more will likely take the place of passwords and metal keys.*

**The iRobot Pro stands about 4 feet high and is designed to be run from a Web site anywhere in the world. It gives the user a chance to "be" wherever the robot is, seeing what it sees and hearing what it hears.**

Since robots generally have to start at the pixel level in identifying an image, let's take a look at how they eventually come to know what they are looking at. Although there are several approaches that robots use to analyze digital images, their common goal is to highlight important image features, such as doorways, staircases, and walls.

One method, called edge extraction, is done by making potentially billions of comparisons between the pixels within each picture. Edge extraction is a funny-sounding name, but what it means is that the robot is trying to outline all the edges of the various objects in a particular picture.

One way to understand this is to do some sketching with paper and pencil. Stand at the door of your bedroom and draw just the outline of each object you see. Don't worry about making it perfect. When you finish, give the paper to someone else. From the outlines they will be able to recognize a bed, perhaps, or a desk, a window, or closet door.

**Urbie, the Urban Surveillance robot, was designed to climb stairs by flipping the pointed rubber treads forward to span the distance between each stair tread.**

This is exactly what a robot tries to do with edge extraction, except it must find the edges by comparing each pixel in an image with all of the pixel's neighbors. Wherever the neighboring pixels are sharply different in shading—say, a dark pixel next to a light one—the edge of an object might have been found.

To understand this better, find a brick or block of wood and place it in the sun outside. Now look at the top and the side facing you. Do you see how one surface looks darker than the other, even though you know they are the same color? This is because of the way light is falling on the brick. Now focus on where those two surfaces meet. Do you see how the shading changes from lighter to darker right at the edge? It is this sort of difference in shading that a robot is looking for with edge extraction. When it finds shading changes like this, it draws a line. Doing this many times creates outlines of the objects in the image just like the drawing you made earlier of your bedroom.

From these outlines, the robot then must decide what it has found. It does this by comparing the various outlined shapes to the shapes it has stored in its memory. If there is a match, then the robot knows what it is looking at and can decide what to do.

Here we see what Urbie the robot sees. Do you understand the picture? Look carefully and you will see a set of stairs Urbie has outlined in the drawing through the process of edge detection.

## HEAR, HEAR!

When the first robot became available for commercial use in 1961, the only way to communicate with it was electronically. All of its commands were stored on a drum of magnetic memory, and once the robot was turned on, those commands were what ran the machine.

In today's world, many industrial robots still operate in much the same way. And this is fine for the robot that spends its life on the

23

One of the latest developments in CMU's Nursebot project, Pearl is shown here by the entrance to a nursing home where she is being tested.

assembly line and has little contact with humans. But as robots become more versatile, it is often necessary for them to interact directly with their human masters.

We could spend time typing our commands on keyboards robots might carry with them, but this is quite tedious. Why shouldn't we just talk to them? What could be more natural than having a conversation?

## SOUNDS SIMPLE

As you might expect, just because it seems natural to us doesn't mean it's easy for a robot to do. In fact, both speech and voice recognition by machine have been the subjects of intense scientific research for several decades.

First of all, however, we should be clear that voice recognition and speech recognition are actually two separate things. Voice recognition is part of the biometrics field we examined earlier. It is about recognizing the particular person who owns the voice that is speaking. Speech recognition is about understanding the meaning of what someone is saying to you.

## SPEAK UP

Voice recognition systems have actually been commercially available for a few years now. The real challenge begins with speech recogni-

## Patterned Sound

*Like facial structures, voice patterns are unique to each of us. Voice patterns are groupings of sound waves emanating from our vocal cords, coming up the throat and out the mouth and nose. Each of these elements—vocal cords, throat, mouth, and nose—contributes to the tone of the voice. And since each element is different from person to person, everyone's voice is at least slightly different from everyone else's.*

*The face-recognition robot we saw earlier could also use voice recognition to be doubly sure about the person in front of it. A person trying to enter the building would not only have to stop and have his or her face identified, but also be required to say a few words to the robot. The robot would then record the words, analyze the voice's sound-wave pattern, and compare it to the voice patterns in its memory. If there is a match, the robot would then allow the person to enter.*

**The voice pattern is a complex set of sound waves unique to each person.**

tion, when robots must recognize not just your voice, but what you are saying.

Let's think about speech. The first thing you might notice is that everyone uses it differently. Some of your friends talk fast. Some talk slow. Some speak with long pauses. And some put hardly any space between their words at all. Yet somehow our brain manages to understand what the speaker is saying.

Once again, what is very natural to us can be very difficult for a machine. A brief example might help you appreciate one of the

26

problems. Turn on your television or radio and find a foreign-language program. Depending on where you live, there may be Spanish radio stations, French or Japanese TV programs, or many others. Find a language you are unfamiliar with.

Concentrate on listening to spoken words rather than music. You may begin to sense a certain rhythm to the sounds, but it is unlikely you will be able to tell exactly where one word ends and another begins. Now think about how you speak. Doesn't the ending sound of one word run into and slightly change the beginning sound of the next one? In every language, native speakers tend to run the words together.

Knowing where one word ends and another begins is very hard for a machine to determine because often there is no noticeable break between them. That is why many current speech recognition systems still require you to make a small stop between each word. Try talking that way and you will see how artificial and machine-like you sound.

Word separation is only one of the many challenges of speech recognition. What about different accents? Someone who has grown up in northern Maine, for example, has a very different way of speaking than someone who grew up in southern Mississippi. And what about homonyms? Homonyms are words that are spelled differently and have different meanings, but sound the same, like "so" and "sew," "sight" and "site," or "hair" and "hare." If you told a robot waiter

**Robots are learning to fly. Researchers at the University of Southern California are studying what it takes for an airborne robot, in the form of a helicopter, to stay aloft and travel through its environment.**

27

"There's a hair in my soup," would it think there was a rabbit in your soup?

As you can see, machine recognition of spoken language has many complex problems to solve. Despite these, progress is being made. Many companies have basic speech-understanding systems that answer their phones. In these cases you can choose a phone menu selection by just saying that number aloud instead of pressing the phone's number pad.

There are also systems becoming available for your PC that will take your spoken words and convert them into typed text. Perhaps keyboards will soon disappear altogether as we become able to speak to our computers and robots and have them speak back.

## MAKING CONTACT

When you look at our bodies and how we function, it is not hard to see why the first robots introduced, and still the most widely used robots today, are modeled after the human arm. Our arm and hand systems are capable of performing a broad range of tasks. They lift, pull, push, grip, and touch, among other things. They are also capable of incredibly fine and subtle movements, such as those needed by a jeweler, as well as gross and powerful actions, like those used by a weightlifter or boxer.

28

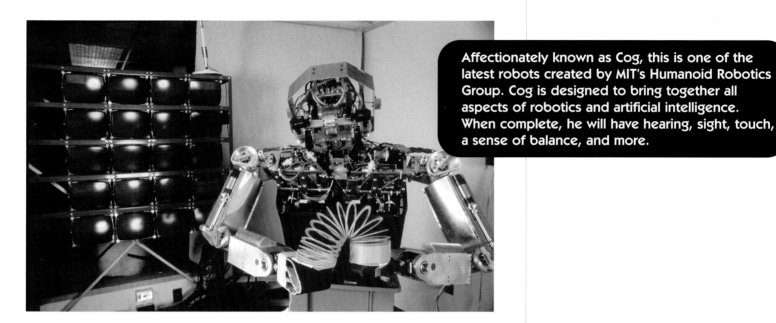

Affectionately known as Cog, this is one of the latest robots created by MIT's Humanoid Robotics Group. Cog is designed to bring together all aspects of robotics and artificial intelligence. When complete, he will have hearing, sight, touch, a sense of balance, and more.

However, until fairly recently, these robot arms had one very significant shortcoming. They lacked a sense of touch. The study of touch and the related topic of force feedback, which we will examine shortly, are part of a field of study called haptics. The word "haptics" comes from a Greek word, *haptesthai*, meaning "to touch."

What good is touch? Let's go back to the glass experiment we did earlier. With the glass of juice in front of you once again, slide your hand out and grab the glass. How did you know when to close your

## I'm Touched

It is interesting to note that of all the human senses, touch is the only one for which no direct mechanism in the human body has yet been identified. For sight we have eyes; for hearing, ears; for taste, taste buds; and for smell, olfactory receptors. But there is as yet nothing that scientists can point to in the skin and say, "This causes touch to be felt."

This mystery of touch, however, may soon be a thing of the past. Scientists at Columbia University are now testing a molecular model of touch that involves certain chemical ion channels on the surfaces of skin cells. Apparently, pressure opens these channels, allowing charged ions to enter a cell. These, in turn, create an electrical impulse that passes along the nerves to the brain, causing us to feel the contact.

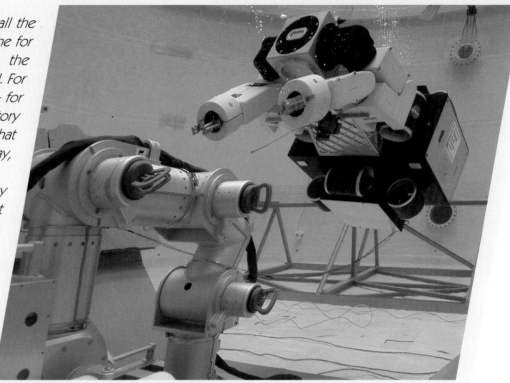

The Space Systems Lab (SSL) at the University of Maryland built the Ranger Neutral Buoyancy Vehicle shown above to demonstrate the capabilities of a free-flying telerobot to help with tasks on the space station. It has four manipulators and is designed to help with refueling, instrument package replacement, worksite preparation, and various other space-based tasks outside the station. Here it is approaching a device in a model of the Shuttle cargo bay in SSL's neutral buoyancy test tank.

hand? The answer is obvious: when you felt your fingers contacting the glass.

Now pick it up. Do you feel how your fingers tighten on the glass and don't let it slip? Without touch, you would not know how much pressure to apply. Now think of screwing in a lightbulb. If you didn't have a sense of touch, you just might squeeze the ultra-thin glass and shatter it in your hand.

Similarly, without touch, a robot would simply have to guess at how much pressure to use when handling an object. This is clearly not a problem if the robot works on a factory assembly line and deals with the same parts every day. In this case, the strength of the robot's grip could be set at a single level that works for the task it is doing.

However, what might happen when robots enter the world of humans? Here the tasks could vary tremendously, from changing light-bulbs to picking up concrete blocks. These robots need the varying sensitivity that the sense of touch brings.

For this reason, as the role of robots expands, robot builders have been adding various pressure-sensitive sensors to the robot's growing arsenal of devices used to sense the world around it. Scientists are even developing pressure-sensitive skins to coat the arms of a robot, so it can feel when it bumps into something, just the way we do when we brush against a table or a wall.

## FEEDING BACK THE FORCE

Force feedback is also a key part of the haptic world of robots and is particularly important in telerobotics, the direct human control of robots at a distance. That distance can be many miles, as when scientists directed the *Sojourner* on Mars, or only a few feet, as in robotic heart surgery.

To know what is meant by force feedback, you need only to remember the last time you went to a video arcade. Many simulation games nowadays use force feedback to increase the feeling of realism. Car race games almost all have some sort of force feedback. Do you remember how the steering wheel became harder and harder to steer as your car went faster? Or how the steering wheel vibrated when your car drove off the track?

The forces created by the car's wheels on the virtual roadway imitate the forces you might feel in a real car. The game directs those forces back to the steering wheel so you feel physically in contact with the road.

## LONG-DISTANCE ROBOTS

In telerobotics, the force feedback process is similar, except that the forces you feel come from the robot doing something in the real world. While this haptic feedback is not necessary in all telerobotic

MASTER CONTROLLERS

SERVO MANIPULATOR
CONTROL BOXES

3D-TV MONITOR

COLOR
PROJECTION
MONITOR

24" COLOR
MONITOR

BLACK AND WHITE
MONITORS

CRT GRAPHIC
DISPLAY

CAMERA CONTROL
PANEL

TRANSPORTER
CONTROL PANEL

L CONTROL
PANEL

This is an elaborate telerobotic control station created at Oak Ridge National Laboratory. The operator uses the arms coming down over her shoulders to directly control the hands and arms of a robot in another location.

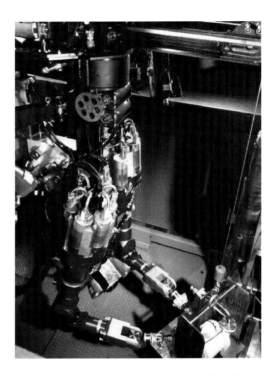

This telerobot could be controlled by the base station at left. An operator could stay safe while the robot is handling highly dangerous chemicals or radioactive materials.

33

## Direct Brain Control

In an experiment that seems straight from science fiction, scientists at Duke University have created the most advanced telerobotic interface yet: direct brain control.

Researchers there implanted ninety-six extremely fine electrodes directly into an owl monkey's brain. The electrical activity from the monkey's brain was then fed into a computer connected to a set of robotic arms six hundred miles away in a lab at the Massachusetts Institute of Technology (MIT). When the monkey reached for food, the robot arms moved in just the same way.

While we are still a long way from connecting human brains to robots in this fashion, this new development promises to revolutionize how people with severe paralysis, or people who have lost limbs, can participate in the world. Just by thinking, their brains would be able to directly control their wheelchairs, for example, or their robotic arms and legs.

**Researchers at Duke University have shown by implanting up to 96 electrodes into an owl monkey's brain that direct brain to machine interface is possible.**

applications, such as the *Sojourner* Mars mission, it is paramount in any task where touch is essential for success. In surgery, for example, if a doctor cannot feel the scalpel making contact, he may cut too far too fast before becoming aware of the damage done.

In the case of telerobotic heart surgery, the surgeon sits at a console that consists of hand controls to operate the microsized surgical tools, and a monitor to see what the tools are doing. The robotic tools and camera are inserted inside the heart via a connecting artery.

As the surgical tools contact the inner surface of the heart, the haptic, or touch feedback, data are sent back to the human-sized control system, creating a sense of resistance against the surgeon's hand and fingers. Thus the doctor can literally feel what is going on inside the heart, even though he has no actual physical contact with it. Such approaches to surgery greatly reduce the trauma to heart patients and thus speed the process of recovery.

Telerobots come in many forms, and a variety of different interfaces are used to control them. The Naval Ocean Systems Center, for example, has created a series of flying and driving tele-operated surveillance robots. Operators must don virtual-reality headsets and operate a full set of controls to maneuver these robots through the world.

Scientists at Carnegie Mellon University (CMU), however, took a different and simpler approach to interfacing with their telerobot, which is named Xavier. Xavier looks like a big black and silver can and roams the halls of the CMU robot lab on missions he receives from people over the Internet. Anyone can log onto his site, see what he sees, and then send him down the hall to someone's office. You can even make him tell a knock-knock joke when he arrives at his destination.

Not only scientists can control robots over the Web. You can, too. Xavier is a robot that roams the halls of the CMU Robotics Institute, and part of the time he can be accessed by anybody with a connection to the Internet.

## GETTING SMART

So far we have examined the first part of the basic robotic cycle of sense-think-act. The sense-think-act cycle lies at the heart of all robot-

Researchers at the Northeastern University Marine Science Center have created an underwater robot based on the body of a lobster. It will be used for underwater sensing along ocean shores and rivers.

ic behaviors. It is going on all the time, allowing the robot to stay aware of its outside world and to take action when necessary.

It is even happening while the robot is actively doing something. For example, if a robot needs to pick up a wooden block, it will continually check with its sensors that its hand is moving toward contact, make an assessment about whether everything is going according to plan, and correct the motion if needed, until the block has been lifted to its new location.

36

This repeating of the sense-think-act cycle is called closed loop control. This means that the results of one repetition of the basic robotic cycle directly affect the next cycle.

## UNEASY THOUGHTS

When it comes to robot intelligence, we humans seem unsure of how we feel about it. In science-fiction films, like *The Terminator*, or *The Matrix*, for example, robots are regularly portrayed as an enemy of the human race, out to destroy us and take our place.

### Robot Destiny

The word "Kismet" means "fate" or "destiny." It is also the name of a very emotional robot at the MIT Robotics Lab. Kismet is a robot head and shoulders complete with eyes, lips, and ears, each of which move based on Kismet's emotional state. For example, when Kismet sees its favorite toy waved in front of its face, its eyes follow the toy and open wide in excitement, while it smiles and perks up its ears. If Kismet has nothing to do, the eyes droop, the mouth and ears go slack, and the head tips downward.

Researchers at MIT, however, aren't fooled into thinking that these visible changes reflect true feelings. They know that Kismet's responses are directly programmed into its software. What interests them is the ease with which humans can relate to Kismet because of this emotional interface. They feel that for robots to be successfully integrated into our lives, developing such a natural way to relate to them will be absolutely necessary.

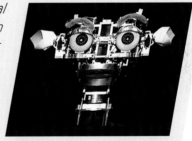

**With its multitude of expressions, Kismet seems almost human.**

**Robots range from very large industrial systems to the very tiny. Here we see two robots created at Sandia Laboratories that are only slightly larger than a penny.**

Given this unease, perhaps we should ask why we feel the need for intelligent robots in the first place. This is not as silly a question as it may sound. After years of failing to create intelligent robots, some researchers have taken a decidedly different approach to robotics and are deliberately designing what they call "stupid robots." These are robots that are capable of doing just one or two tasks really well and that are totally ignorant of anything else.

It is thought that groups of these limited-function robots might be able to work together to perform a more complicated task. For example, if you wanted to build a house, you might use some robots that know only how to dig a hole for the foundation, other robots that can pour concrete, and still other robots that can only erect a wall. Together they can make a building, and the incredible difficulties of creating a robot smart enough to do it all can be sidestepped altogether.

While it is not hard to imagine a collection of robots working together on a construction site, it doesn't seem practical for either the home or the office. At home you would need one robot that knew how to fetch the drinks, another that specialized in clearing the table, a third to clean the floor, a fourth to cut the grass, and so on. It is not hard to see that you would soon be stumbling over a number of these "stupid robots" everywhere you turned.

In addition, as more and more robots become available, there will be a growing need to relate to robots easily and in a familiar man-

ner, a task that requires a great deal more brain power. We as humans are keenly attuned to each other's facial expressions and emotional states. We talk to one another using words and body language. It's all very natural. Why shouldn't we be able to use this set of well-developed communications strategies with our robots?

## WHAT'S INSIDE

Amazingly enough, most robots' brains consist of nothing more than the computer chips used in PCs or their more powerful workstation cousins. This is the physical technology, like the neurons in our brains, that supports the "think" portion of a robot's sense-think-act cycle.

These computer chips by themselves, however, are essentially worthless until there is software that tells them what to do. The power and speed of the chip clearly can make a difference in a robot's abilities, but it is the software that creates what we might think of as the robot's mind. The software coordinates all the sensor input signals, develops a plan of action, and then issues commands to the robotic "muscles" known as actuators.

Computer software is created by using what are called programming languages. There are many such languages, including Basic, C++, Java, Pascal, and LISP. You have probably heard of some of these. Unless you have been following developments in robotics and artificial intelligence, however, you probably don't know much about LISP.

Robots get around on wheels, legs, pistons, and more. This robot, created by researchers at Lawrence Livermore National Laboratories, uses archimedes screws. The powerful screws propel this robot sideways like a crab.

39

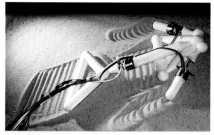

In an amazing experiment in robot design, these two odd-looking specimens were created from start to finish by other robots. They were even manufactured robotically with humans serving only to snap the final parts together. The goal of the project was to create robot designs that could move across a flat surface on their own. What resulted was a series of effective designs that no human would have thought of.

## Fuzzy Logic

*Logic and logical reasoning allow us to state that something is definitely true or absolutely false. But what is fuzzy logic? Actually, you use fuzzy logic every day with words like "nearly," "almost," "not quite," and "some." Let's say you are looking in the garage for your scooter and you catch a glimpse of something silvery behind the car. You can't be sure, but it seems to be "almost" the same color as your scooter. So you go over and check. Fuzzy logic has just allowed you to make a decision and take action, even though you weren't completely certain you were right.*

*Computer scientists and logicians have developed fuzzy logic systems that now permit this sort of approximate reasoning in computers. In fact, these systems are being used in many areas, including household appliances and automobiles. Some scientists think that fuzzy logic may hold the key to creating real robotic intelligence.*

The primary strength of LISP is its ability to represent logical reasoning through sets of "if/then" rules. By this we mean, *if* condition 1 is true, *then* do action 1. An example might be, *if* you see a glass of juice, *then* pick it up and drink it. The LISP language allows programmers to rapidly define many such separate as well as interconnected logical conditions and actions. Since LISP can imitate this form of logical reasoning, it is widely used to develop and test various theories of robotic intelligence.

It is also at the software level that the majority of the most difficult problems in robotics are encountered. This is largely due to how lit-

tle we really know about ourselves. How can we create robotic intelligence or robotic learning, for example, when we don't know how our own minds learn and think?

Through creating new hypotheses and testing them in software on the latest robots, researchers are making slow progress. However, no one yet knows how robotic intelligence will arise. It might come from a breakthrough in neuroscience research or perhaps through some unique combination of the latest theories of intelligence using neural nets, fuzzy logic, and new biocomputer chips that incorporate human or animal neurons into their silicon structure. Or maybe it will arrive, as we did, through some form of evolution.

## WHERE THE ACTION IS

The final phase of the robotic behavioral cycle is where the action takes place. This is where the robotic muscles, known as actuators, move the hands, arms, legs, wheels, or other movable parts in response to commands from the computer processor. Actuators are mechanical devices that can be as large as the hydraulic systems used in giant bucket loaders or as tiny as a microelectronic motor smaller than a human hair. The size of the actuator depends on the size of the parts it must move.

Most actuators operate much like the motors found in battery-operated toys. Most often, they turn gears that rotate wheels, flex

### Neural Networks

*Neural networks were inspired by the hardware of our own brains, the nerves. Neural nets, as they are known, are the digital world's attempt to imitate the way sets of nerves in the brain work together to come to some sort of conclusion. They are mathematically complex and are particularly useful in object recognition. In fact, they can quickly recognize objects in images even if the images are faint and blurry.*

41

## New Muscles

There is a new kind of "muscle" being developed that has no moving parts at all. It is called an electroactive polymer (EAP). EAPs are very light, strong, and inexpensive plastic materials that change form in predictable ways when an electrical charge is sent through them. When the charge is removed, the material snaps back to its original shape.

Scientists at NASA's Jet Propulsion Lab have built a robotic arm with four EAP "fingers" capable of gripping and lifting small objects. They have also created a small EAP windshield wiper to scrape planetary dust from sensors as it is kicked up by a rover's wheels.

EAPs look very promising, but they have one substantial drawback that researchers are trying to correct: They can change form and snap back only a limited number of times because the material gradually loses its ability to respond to the electrical charges.

**Muscles without mechanics. Scientists have discovered a family of materials that change shape when given an electric charge. These materials are extremely lightweight, strong, and may one day be used to gather rock samples on another planet.**

joints, or operate hydraulic pumps that extend and retract pistons. Without actuators, a robot could do nothing but sense and think.

Although scientists are researching new kinds of actuators such as the EAP systems, how to use actuators in robots is well understood. Essentially, each moving part in a robot needs a minimum of one actuator for each direction of movement.

For example, if you were making a robotic wrist that works like a human one, it would need to be able to rotate (as our wrists do when we turn a screwdriver), move up and down (as when we wave our hand), and slide from side to side (as when we twist open a bottle). Thus, a minimum of three actuators would be needed.

The number of actuators that any robot can use depends on two things: the number of moving parts in the robot, and the ability of the robot's software and hardware to properly control that number of actuators to do the job required, whether it's placing a computer chip on a circuit board, welding an automobile body, or rolling over the surface of a distant planet.

## ACTING UP

Actuators themselves are just a small part of the final phase of the sense-think-act cycle. The real difficulties for robot builders lie in coordinating all the actuators to produce a desired physical behavior. As an example, let's look at how we walk.

Humans who are physically capable don't even think about how to walk after they have reached the age of two or three. It's just done naturally. The process of walking, however, particularly on two legs, is a lot more complex than it looks.

To demonstrate this, stand up and center your weight over both legs. Be as sensitive as you can be to what your body is doing. Can

Talk about jumping for joy! Researchers at Sandia National Laboratories in New Mexico have created a unique set of robots that get around by hopping from place to place. Some can jump as high as 30 feet and could cover a lot of ground if used to explore low-gravity planets like Mars.

43

you feel what it takes to stay vertically balanced? This seemingly relaxed position is actually a riot of muscular activities. In each joint, from your toes to your neck, your body is sensing position and movement and making constant micro adjustments with your muscles so you don't fall over.

Now take a couple of steps. Can you feel how you first tilt your torso slightly forward? This puts you off balance, so your foot steps ahead to catch up, placing itself under the moving weight of your body. When you think about it, walking and running are a lot like controlled falling.

As you can see, balancing and walking are very subtle and difficult to understand. It was only very recently that some experimental robots, like Honda's new humanoid robot, could perform these actions.

In fact, the process of bipedal (two-legged) walking has been under intense scientific study at places like the MIT Leg Laboratory for nearly two decades. Since the lab's beginning in 1982, scientists at MIT have developed single-legged balancers, stiff-legged walkers, pogo-stick hoppers, walkers with primitive feet, and even systems capable of elementary gymnastics. The progress has been steady, and from what the scientists have learned, they are now constructing a multijointed, humanoid, bipedal walker.

Isn't it surprising to think that something we all do so easily could take twenty years to understand? These actions, however, are only one

such complex behavior that the "act" phase of the robotic cycle must know how to handle. There are many more. Think of the incredible variety of movements that human hands and fingers can make: opening bottles, screwing in lightbulbs, grasping and lifting, and much more. And what about robots that swim like fish or move like other animals? Each of these forms of movement must be meticulously analyzed to understand what sorts of actions the various actuators controlling a robot's moving parts must make.

When you understand the difficulties, it is really no wonder that walking, swimming, and flying robots are only now entering our world.

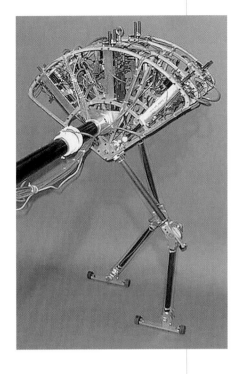

Known as Spring Flamingo because of its birdlike leg structure, this robot, created at the MIT Leg Lab, was their first to use feet and active ankles.

## FUTUREBOTS

For over forty years, scientists have been methodically laying down the foundations for the field of robotics, increasing the capabilities of each phase of the robot's sense-think-act cycle. Cameras, microphones, artificial skin and touch receptors, and other sensory devices allow today's robots to more fully sense their world. Continuing

**Created by Tiger Electronics, i-Cybie is one of the growing number of very sophisticated robots that are finding their way into the home as both toys and robotic companions.**

improvements in software help robots understand more clearly what they are perceiving and make more intelligent decisions and plans about what to do. And greater understanding of complex physical motions lets robots move more naturally and take on more tasks in our human-oriented world.

Even though robotics can still be considered in its infancy, there is little doubt that increasingly capable robots will play an ever larger role in our lives. We can soon expect to have our grass cut by robotic lawn mowers and rugs cleaned by robotic vacuum systems. Our refrigerators may shortly order our food for us as it runs out, and our washing machines will likely set their cycles based on the clothes they sense in their tubs. In addition, toys like Aibo, Poo-Chi, and My Real Baby will become ever more sophisticated playmates and companions.

Whether real intelligence or self-awareness, as explored in science fiction, will ever arise in future robots is anybody's guess. Some scientists think that it might require fifty more years of intense research, while others feel we will never reach that goal. However it turns out, robotics can be seen as something far grander than just a way to build ever-smarter machines. At its heart, it is a science that is helping us unravel the deepest mysteries of what it means to be human.

# RESOURCES

There are many robot resources on the Web. Try starting with these:

**MIT Leg Laboratory**
www.ai.mit.edu/projects/leglab/home-main.html

**MIT Artificial Intelligence Laboratory**
www.ai.mit.edu

**Humanoid Robotics Group**
www.ai.mit.edu/projects/humanoid-robotics-group

**NASA/Jet Propulsion Lab Robotics**
robotics.jpl.nasa.gov

**Intelligent Systems & Robotic Center**
www.sandia.gov/isrc

**Space Systems Laboratory at the University of Maryland**
www.ssl.umd.edu

**Lawrence Livermore National Laboratory/Automation & Intelligent Systems**
www.llnl.gov/automation-robotics

**The Robotics Institute/Carnegie Mellon University**
www.ri.cmu.edu

**Robotics at Space and Naval Warfare Systems Center, San Diego**
www.nosc.mil/robots

# INDEX